PROMPT

The Art of Asking AI

Suraj Sheikh

PROMPT— The Art Of Asking AI

Second Edition, 2025

ISBN: 978-93-342-9851-2

Published by learndek.com
India.

Trademarks

OpenAI®, ChatGPT®, DALL·E®, GPT-4®, GitHub®, Copilot®, MidJourney™, Stable Diffusion™, Gemini™, and all related marks and logos are trademarks or registered trademarks of their respective owners. Any other product names, brand names, or logos mentioned in this book remain the property of their rightful holders and are used solely for identification and explanatory purposes; no endorsement is implied.

Disclaimer

Every effort has been made to ensure that the information in this book is accurate and complete. However, the author and publisher assume no responsibility for errors, omissions, or damages resulting from the use of the information herein. All prompt samples are provided "as is" and without warranty of any kind.

For permissions, bulk orders, or instructor resources, please contact: suraj.sheikh@aol.in

"Clear prompts craft precise answers; precise answers unlock remarkable outcomes."

— *from the Preface to* ***PROMPT: The Art of Asking AI***

Acknowledgement:

Writing **PROMPT – The Art of Asking AI** has been a collective endeavor disguised as a solitary pursuit. I owe my deepest gratitude to the peers, mentors, and collaborators who challenged every draft, shared their edge-case prompts, and reminded me that curiosity is the sharpest tool in any engineer's kit.

To the early readers and workshop participants who stress-tested these chapters with real-world problems—your questions turned theory into practice.

To my family and friends: thank you for tolerating conversations that began with "One more experiment..." and stretched long past midnight. Your patience fueled every revision.

A special salute to the open-source communities—Python, Java, JavaScript, Rust, and beyond—whose relentless generosity set the standard for knowledge-sharing. Your repos, forums, and late-night code reviews proved that progress is a team sport.

And finally, to you, the reader: your trust is the reason these pages exist. May the prompts you craft unlock possibilities none of us have imagined yet.

About Author

Suraj Sheikh is a software architect, educator, and relentless tinkerer who believes technology should feel less like a riddle and more like a well-told story. Over the past decade he has engineered high-throughput back-end systems, wrangled cloud-native platforms, and guided enterprise teams in both Java and modern Python—always with one eye on elegance and the other on practicality.

Suraj's fascination with language models began when he noticed that the hardest part of solving complex problems was no longer writing code, but asking the right question. That insight led him to prompt engineering, where syntax meets psychology. Today he designs AI-driven solutions for data-rich organizations and teaches developers how to turn a single sentence into a working prototype.

Outside the terminal you might find him stargazing, debating the paradoxes of time travel, or hiking remote trails in search of unspoiled night skies. He mentors young engineers through open-source projects and conference workshops, helping them evolve from coders into systems thinkers.

PROMPT — The Art of Asking AI Anything is Suraj's tribute to the communities that taught him to learn out loud and share without hesitation. He hopes every page equips you to converse with machines as confidently as you collaborate with humans—and to build futures that, just yesterday, felt out of reach.

To my parents—

for your unwavering love, quiet strength, and constant belief in my dreams.

This book is possible because of you.

TABLE OF CONTENTS

INTRODUCTION

Why Prompts Matter

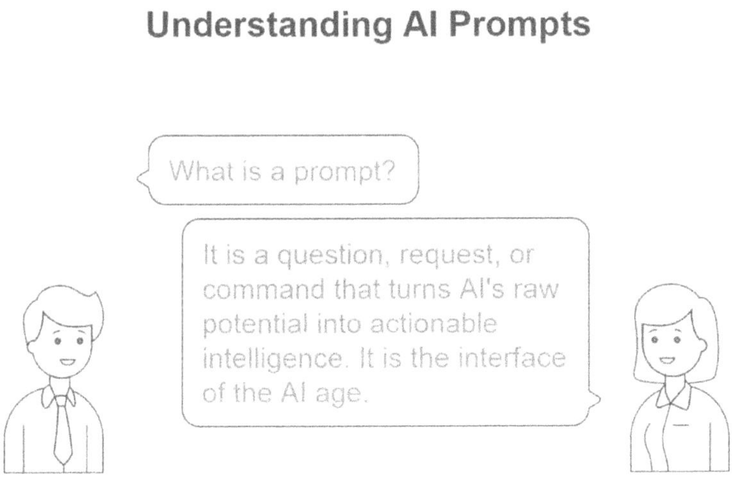

Imagine standing on a shoreline where every grain of sand is a snippet of human knowledge: literature, mathematics, medicine, music, cooking, quantum physics, ancient myths, and yesterday's memes. Modern AI models—particularly large language models (LLMs)—have sifted through those sands to learn patterns, styles, and relationships. Yet they remain silent until someone frames the right question. A *prompt* is that question, request, or command. It is the key that turns raw potential into actionable intelligence.

Throughout history, invention bloomed around new interfaces—alphabets, printing presses, keyboards, GUIs. Prompts are the interface of the AI age. Crafting them well determines whether you receive a vague surf-report or a perfectly timed forecast down to each breaking wave. Good prompts:

- **Specify intent** (what you want)
- **Set context** (what the model should know or emulate)
- **Define format** (how the answer should look)
- **Add constraints** (rules that keep the output useful)

Prompt Template #1 – Basic Four-Part Prompt

Role: *"You are a cybersecurity analyst."*

Task: *"Summarize the attached log for threats."*
Format: *"Return a Markdown table with columns: Threat, Severity, Suggested Fix."*
Constraints: *"Limit to 200 words. If no threats, say 'None.'"*

A single sentence like, "Explain photosynthesis," exposes only a sliver of AI's capacity. A well-composed prompt coaxes the model to reason, self-check, and respond at exactly the depth you need—whether you're a fifth-grader preparing a science fair project or a botanist drafting a grant proposal.

How This Book Will Change the Way You Use AI

Most users treat AI like a novelty search engine. They ask once and hope for magic. You, however, are about to become a *prompt engineer*—someone who crafts systematic, reliable instructions that turn AI into:

- **A writing collaborator:** generating first drafts, stylistic rewrites, or sensitivity edits in minutes.
- **A code assistant:** fixing bugs, documenting functions, and generating unit tests while you sleep.
- **A data analyst:** summarizing CSVs, detecting anomalies, and proposing visualizations.
- **An idea accelerator:** brainstorming startup concepts, marketing slogans, or lesson plans without limit.

After this chapter—and the 11 that follow—you will be able to:

1. **Design prompt frameworks** that consistently deliver predictable, high-quality results.

2. **Diagnose and debug** bad outputs by tweaking temperature, context length, or instruction order.
3. **Chain prompts into workflows**, automating tasks that once required whole teams.
4. **Guard against bias and hallucination**, keeping AI grounded in facts and ethics.

Meet Your New Creative Partner: The Model

LLMs like **GPT-4-Turbo**, **Claude 3**, and **Gemini Ultra** are text machines; image models like **DALL·E 3** and **MidJourney v6** paint pictures with pixels. Underneath, each model is a giant neural network trained to predict the next token—word fragments, image patches, or code symbols—based on trillions of prior examples.

A Lightning Tour Under the Hood

Layer	What It Does	Why It Matters to Prompting
Embedding	Converts words or pixels into vectors	Similar concepts sit near each other; synonyms help or hurt.
Attention	Lets the model focus on relevant parts of the context	Longer prompts can mislead if key instructions appear too early or too late.
Feed-Forward Blocks	Combine signals to predict the next token	Small temperature tweaks here change creativity.
Output Decoding	Transforms vectors back into human-readable text or images	Controls like top-p or frequency penalty shape final style.

When you ask the model, "Draft an email apologizing for a late invoice," the request passes through these layers. Each layer's behavior can be steered—subtly or dramatically—by how you phrase the prompt.

A Short Story: The Tale of Two Designers

Ada and Ben both need an executive summary for a 45-page market report.

- Ada writes: *"Summarize this report."* She receives a 600-word generic overview.
- Ben writes: *"You are a C-suite market analyst. Summarize the attached PDF for a busy CEO. Use three bullet points on opportunities, two on risks, and end with a one-sentence recommendation."* He receives a crisp, 120-word brief that the CEO forwards to the board.

Same model, same document, radically different outcomes—all due to prompting.

Additional Subtitles for Depth and Clarity

The Four Pillars of Prompt Engineering

1. **Role Framing** – Assigning the model an identity or perspective.

2. **Task Clarity** – Detailing exactly what you want done.
3. **Format Precision** – Specifying tables, bullet lists, JSON, DOCX, or HTML.
4. **Constraint Guardrails** – Setting limits on length, tone, or factual references.

Common Myths Debunked

- **Myth**: "Just ask AI anything."
  Reality: Vague prompts waste tokens and time.
- **Myth**: "More context is always better."
  Reality: Excess context can bury key instructions beyond the model's focus window.
- **Myth**: "Temperature zero guarantees accuracy."
- **Reality**: It reduces randomness but does not ensure factual answers; checking sources is still required.

A Quick Exercise: Your First Prompt Makeover

1. **Write a simple request:** *"Tell me about renewable energy."*
2. **Apply the Four Pillars:**
    - **Role:** *"You are an energy policy advisor."*
    - **Task/Goal:** *"Draft an executive brief on the top three renewable sources for 2030."*
    - **Format:** *"Return a Markdown bullet list, 75 words max per bullet."*
    - **Constraints:** *"Cite one reputable source link per bullet."*
3. **Send the improved prompt** and compare outputs.

Result Template

- **Solar** – 75 words... (Source: IEA)
- **Wind** – 75 words... (Source: DOE)

- **Green Hydrogen** – 75 words... (Source: BloombergNEF)

Notice how clarity, structure, and constraints channel the model's knowledge into exactly what you need.

Next Steps: Your Journey Through This Book

- **Part I** dives deeper into how AI models think, read, and respond.
- **Part II** explores domain-specific prompting for text, code, images, and multimedia.
- **Part III** reveals advanced techniques such as prompt chaining, role prompting, and zero- vs few-shot prompts.
- **Part IV** teaches you to build complete assistants and workflows that automate knowledge work end-to-end.

At the end of each chapter, you'll find **Prompt Labs**—hands-on exercises to solidify your skills—

and **Real-World Spotlights** featuring professionals who integrated AI prompting into daily workflows.

Final Word

Prompt engineering is not a fad—it's literacy for the AI era. Just as spreadsheets revolutionized accounting and graphic interfaces democratized computing, prompt fluency will redefine what it means to *work*. By the time you finish this book, you won't just *use* AI tools; you'll *design* the very conversations that unlock their power.

Let's begin.

PART I – INSIDE THE MIND OF AI

Chapter 1: What Is an AI Model, Really?

From Search Engines to Thinking Machines

Twenty-five years ago a search engine did one thing: it matched the words you typed to a giant index of web pages. There was no real *understanding*—just keyword Bingo. Yet people marveled because information that once took hours in a library suddenly appeared in seconds.

Fast-forward to the present. You type a single sentence—"Plot twist ideas for a detective novel set on Mars"—and a model replies with original story beats, red herrings, and character arcs within the same breath.

What happened?

1. **Data explosion:** Billions of documents, dialog logs, code repos, and images became the new training ground.
2. **Neural depth:** Networks grew from a handful of layers to hundreds, each layer capturing richer abstractions—syntax in early layers, semantics in middle layers, and stylistic nuance in deeper layers.
3. **Attention mechanism:** Introduced in 2017, attention let models weigh which words (or pixels) mattered most at each step, turning brute-force pattern matching into something that feels eerily like reasoning.

The outcome? A system that no longer just *retrieves* facts but *synthesizes* and *creates*—making "thinking machines" feel much less like science fiction and far more like collaborative partners.

Language Models vs. Image Models

Even seasoned technologists sometimes blur the line between text-only language models (LLMs) and image generators. Let's disentangle them:

- **Language Models (LLMs)** focus on *sequences of tokens*—word fragments, punctuation, snippets of code. Their core skill is predicting the next token, but that simple act unlocks summarization, translation, question answering, joke telling, and code writing.
- **Image Models** work in a *spatial grid*—pixels or latent image patches. They use textual prompts as conditional context, then iteratively refine random noise into an image that matches the prompt.

Which type of AI model should be used for a specific task?

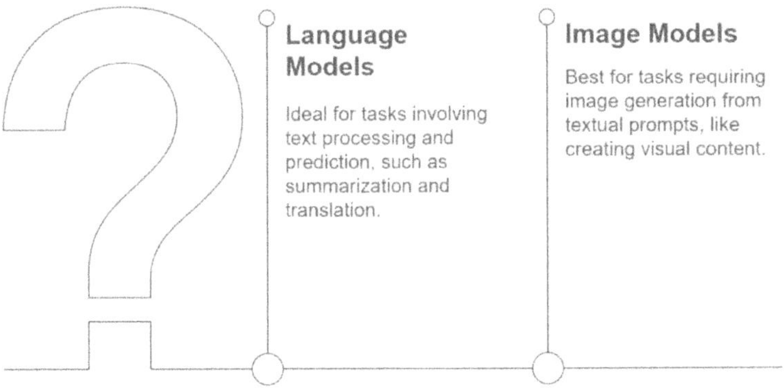

While the input modality differs, the heart of both systems is the same: a probabilistic engine trained to transform *context* into *coherent output*—whether that output is a stanza of poetry or a 1024-pixel masterpiece.

Where They Converge

1. **Embeddings Everywhere**: Both transform raw input into dense numerical vectors that capture meaning.

2. **Attention Guides the Way**: Both weigh relationships—word to word, or pixel patch to prompt token—to decide what matters next.
3. **Prompt Sensitivity**: A single adjective can change tone ("serene mountain" vs "ominous mountain"), just as a single role instruction can shift style ("Act as a high-school teacher...").

Tokens, Training, and How They "Read"

Imagine reading a book through a one-word peephole, seeing only the newest word as you slide the peephole forward. That's how an LLM experiences text during training—it predicts one token at a time, given everything it has seen so far.

Tokens ≠ Words. "Unbelievable" may split into *un-* + *believ-* + *able*. Shorter pieces mean a smaller vocabulary and better handling of new words. But it also means token count—*not* character count—matters when models hit their context limits.

Training in Three Breathless Steps:

1. **Forward Pass** – The model guesses the next token.
2. **Loss Calculation** – It measures how wrong that guess was.
3. **Backward Pass** – It nudges millions of weights to reduce future error.
   This happens over billions of sentences until the model becomes a prediction virtuoso.

How Models "Read" Your Prompt Today:

At inference time, your entire prompt—system role, user instruction, in-context examples—flows in at once. Attention layers search for patterns, weighing each token's relevance to the ones that follow. The model then predicts a token, appends it to the context, and repeats.

> **Prompt Template #2 – Precision Decoder**
> **Role:** *"You are a meticulous historian."*
> **Task:** *"Compare two historical events: the 1929 stock-market crash and the 2008 financial crisis."*
> **Context:** *"Focus on causes, public reaction, and policy response."*
> **Format:** *"Return three numbered sections, each under 120 words."*

Even small tweaks—adding or removing a focus phrase—reshape the prediction landscape, leading to deeper analysis or a shallower overview.

The Myth of AI "Understanding"

People often ask, *"Does the model really understand me?"* If understanding means internal consciousness, the answer is no. But if it means reliably mapping context to output in ways that appear thoughtful, then yes—functionally, it behaves as if it understands. For practical engineering, that functional definition is all that matters.

A quick story: A legal firm fed an LLM thousands of anonymized case briefs and prompted it to draft summaries. Early results were verbose and inconsistent. By tightening prompts with role framing ("Act as a senior appellate attorney"), length limits (450 words), and tone guardrails ("avoid legalese where possible"), the model produced summaries so sharp that junior associates began using them as baselines—saving hours per case.

Parameters, Temperature, and the Human Touch

Two slider bars anyone can grasp yet few truly master:

- **Temperature** controls randomness. Low values (0–0.3) yield deterministic, factual prose. High values (0.7–1.0) spark creativity—and risk nonsense.
- **Top-p (nucleus sampling)** sets a probability threshold, telling the model to consider only the most likely next tokens whose cumulative probability $\leq p$.

Real-world trick: Start with temperature 0.2 for anything procedural (documentation, legal copy). Crank to 0.8 when brainstorming brand slogans or story plots. Pro writers often do both: low-temperature outline, high-temperature ideation, then low-temperature polish.

Limitations and Hallucinations

- **Context Windows:** Most models can juggle only a finite number of tokens. Push past, and early instructions fade from memory.
- **Training Cutoff:** A model last updated in 2023 knows nothing of events in 2025 unless you feed them as context.
- **Hallucination Risk:** Under vague prompts, the model may invent citations or facts. Cure: add constraints—"If unsure, respond: 'I don't have enough info.'"

Closing Takeaways

1. AI models evolved from simple pattern matchers to multi-modal reasoning engines because of data scale, deep networks, and attention.
2. Language and image models share an architecture built on embeddings and

attention, but they operate in different spaces (tokens vs pixels).

3. Knowing token mechanics, temperature, and context limits lets you steer outputs like a seasoned pilot.
4. Clarity beats cleverness. The more explicit your prompt, the more dependable the AI's response.

Prompt Lab #1 – Test Your Understanding

1. Draft a single-sentence prompt asking an LLM to outline a blog post on climate-resilient architecture.
2. Rewrite it using the Four Pillars (role, task, format, constraints). Compare the two outputs.
3. Note differences in structure, depth, and usefulness.

Reflection: Which pillar had the greatest impact and why?

Real-World Spotlight – The MedTech Startup

A health-tech founder used GPT-4 to draft regulatory submissions. Initial prompts produced fluffy marketing copy. By specifying role ("You are a seasoned FDA compliance officer"), adding constraints ("Cite CFR references"), and limiting temperature, the AI produced near-ready sections accepted by their legal team. Time saved: 100+ hours over six weeks.

Chapter 2: How AI Thinks — No, It's Not Magic

Predictive Text, Not Consciousness

Picture a jigsaw puzzle that builds itself, one piece at a time, while referencing billions of completed puzzles. That's what a large language model (LLM) does each time it responds. It isn't dreaming, feeling, or philosophizing. It's engaged in a lightning-fast game of **next-token prediction**.

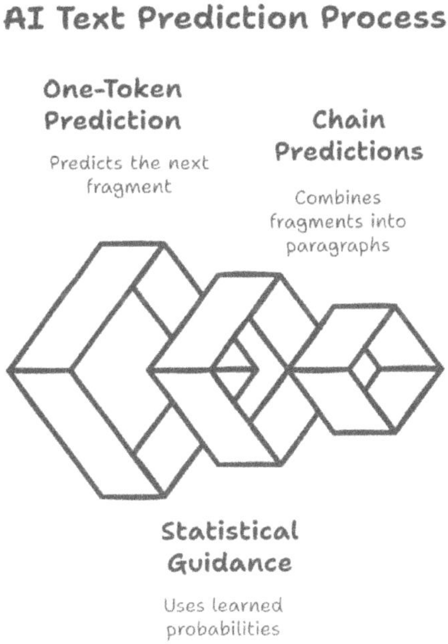

1. **One-Token Horizon** – At any given moment, the model predicts only one fragment—often a sub-word—based on everything before it.
2. **Statistical Intuition** – That prediction is guided by probability distributions learned from oceans of text. The model doesn't "know" Paris is capital of France in the

conscious sense; it has simply seen *Paris* follow *capital of France* so frequently that the link is nearly certain.

3. **Illusion of Insight** – Chain enough micro-predictions together and you get paragraphs that appear thoughtful. It's not thinking—just statistical composition.

Prompt Template #1 – Reality Check

Role: *"You are a fact-checker."*

Task: *"Validate the following claim for accuracy."*

Constraints: *"If insufficient data, reply: 'Not enough evidence.'"*

Use such constraints to keep the model honest and avoid attributing cognition where none exists.

Pattern Recognition on Steroids

Humans excel at spotting small patterns (a face in clouds, a chord progression). An LLM processes

hundreds of billions of data points—entire libraries of patterns far beyond human capacity.

- **Contextual Breadth:** It can connect a 19th-century poem to 21st-century memes because it has read both repeatedly.
- **Cross-Domain Synthesis:** Feed it legal text and it can draft plain-English summaries because legalese patterns coexist with everyday language in its training set.
- **Zero-Shot Generalization:** Ask it to mimic an obscure style and it often can, because it has observed related cues in adjacent texts.

Yet pattern power has limits: novel, unpatterned data (breaking news or esoteric niche topics) can push the model to hallucinate. Always supply clear, recent context when precision matters.

Why It Feels Like AI Understands You

Three psychological cues trick us into sensing real understanding:

1. **Fluency:** Fluid grammar and coherent structure trigger the same trust we place in eloquent human speakers.
2. **Context Recall:** The model references earlier parts of a conversation, creating continuity.
3. **Empathy Simulation:** With the right prompt, it mirrors emotional tone—apologizing, encouraging, or joking on cue.

But remove those cues and the illusion fades. Ask for a step-by-step reasoning chain under strict constraints and you may expose gaps. Example:

> **User Prompt:** "In one sentence: Explain quantum entanglement to a five-year-old."
>
> **LLM:** "It's like having two magic coins that always show the same side, no matter how far apart they are."

That answer *feels* intuitive, yet it glosses over non-local correlations and measurement collapse—fine for a child, risky for research.

Hidden Subroutines: Temperature, Top-p, Penalties

These control knobs shape apparent intelligence:

- **Temperature (0–1):** Lower → deterministic; higher → creative but riskier.
- **Top-p:** Keeps only the top cumulative probability p tokens for sampling; filters unlikely words.
- **Presence/Frequency Penalties:** Discourage repetition, useful for brainstorming.

Real-World Hack: Draft technical docs at *temperature 0.2* for accuracy; switch to *0.8* during ideation sessions.

Attention Windows and Focus Drift

LLMs allocate attention weights per token—but only within a *context window* (e.g., 8k–128k tokens). Place vital instructions at the start **and** end to prevent drift.

Prompt Template #2 – Anchor Instructions

Begin: *"You are a grant-writing specialist..."*

Middle: ...[bulk content]...

End: *"Repeat: This proposal is a two-page NIH R01 summary."*

Chain-of-Thought vs. Direct Answer

Ask the model to *present* reasoning (*"Think step-by-step"*) and you often boost factual accuracy by forcing slower token generation. But be cautious: those reasoning chains can still embed subtle errors. Verification beats blind trust.

Multi-Modal Thinking

Cutting-edge models now process **text + images** or **text + audio**. Prompting changes:

- Add image alt-text descriptions to steer focus.

- Layer text instructions after image uploads to request specific analysis.

Example: *"Here is a screenshot of a Python stack trace (image). Diagnose the root cause and propose a three-line fix."*

Prompt Lab #2 – Steer Creativity and Control

1. **Baseline Prompt:** "Write a short story about lost time."
2. **Experiment:** Generate with temperature 0.2, 0.5, and 0.9. Observe differences in style, risk, and coherence.
3. **Top-p Switch:** Repeat with top-p 0.6 to see vocabulary narrowing effects.
4. **Reflection:** Which setting balances originality and clarity for your purpose?

Closing Takeaways

- AI "thinking" is probabilistic prediction, not consciousness.
- Attention and pattern scale create the illusion of understanding.
- Prompt controls (temperature, top-p, penalties) let you tune between precision and creativity.
- Always anchor critical instructions at both ends of long prompts.
- Chain-of-thought prompts can enhance accuracy but still require verification

Chapter 3: Anatomy of a Response

How AI Breaks Down Your Prompt

Think of your prompt as a screenplay handed to a cast of invisible actors. The script arrives as a single block of text, but backstage the model slices it into discrete **tokens**—tiny word fragments or sub-words. Each token is a cue. The ensemble reads every cue in parallel, deciding who should

speak next, which emotion fits, and how loudly to deliver
each line.

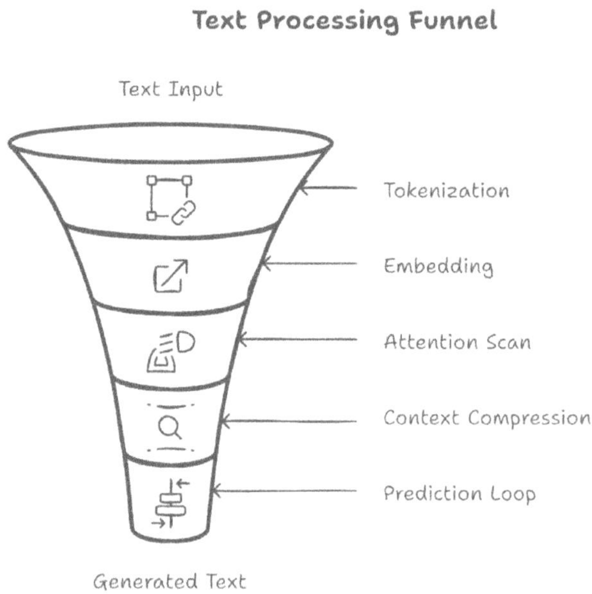

1. **Tokenization:** "Unbelievable" becomes *un*-+ *believ*- + *able*. Shorter, common words remain intact; rare or compound words fracture for efficiency.
2. **Embedding:** Every token converts into a high-dimensional vector—a point in semantic space where "doctor" sits closer to "physician" than to "aardvark."

3. **Attention Scan:** Layers weigh relationships—*Is this instruction? Example? Metadata?* Important tokens glow brighter, telling the model: *Focus here.*
4. **Context Compression:** The model distills hundreds of tokens into compact internal summaries so deeper layers can "remember" what matters as generation proceeds.
5. **Prediction Loop:** Armed with this distilled context, the model predicts the next token, appends it to the running script, re-evaluates attention, and repeats until stop criteria (length, stop word, or user signal) are met.

Prompt Template #1 – Dissect for Clarity

Role: *"You are a medical editor."*
Task: *"Condense the following abstract*

into three bullet points."
Format: *"Use plain English, 40 words max each bullet."*
Constraint: *"If statistical significance isn't mentioned, flag it."*

Notice how each line becomes a high-priority token cluster: role, task, format, constraint. Strategic line breaks amplify their weight in attention.

Reasoning, Rewriting, and Responding

To the user, a response streams as if the model drafts in one continuous burst. Internally, three intertwined processes cycle in milliseconds:

1. **Reasoning (Internal):** A silent chain-of-thought where the model tests micro-hypotheses: *If the user wants 3 bullet points, how do I group findings?* This reasoning rarely appears unless you request it.

2. **Rewriting (Self-Editing):** The model discreetly re-phrases partial thoughts to satisfy style and length constraints before revealing them. It's a real-time editor, pruning verbosity or swapping synonyms to match tone.
3. **Responding (Output):** Finally, the polished token surfaces in your chat UI. The cycle restarts for the next token.

Story Break – The Grant Proposal Miracle

A Ph.D. candidate fed an LLM dense eight-page grant draft. First prompt: *"Edit for clarity."* Result? Shorter sentences but lost nuance. Second prompt: *"You are a peer reviewer. Maintain technical rigor while reducing redundancy by 20 percent."* Result? A tightened, jargon-aware proposal that secured funding. Same model, different internal reasoning triggered by explicit instructions.

Format Awareness: Markdown, HTML, DOCX, and More

Modern models are *format polymaths*. They detect and reproduce structures like:

- **Markdown:** Headings (##), lists (-), code blocks (```).
- **HTML:** <h2>, <p>, <table> tags.
- **DOCX / RTF Hints:** Asking for "Heading 1" or "Normal style" nudges the model to embed Word-friendly markup.
- **LaTeX:** Wrap equations in \(\) for instant math mode.

Prompt Template #2 – Format Lock

"Generate a two-page executive summary **as Markdown** with sections:

Objective, Key Findings, Recommendations. Use numbered sub-headers and end with a single-sentence call to action."

The explicit phrase **as Markdown** tells the model to think in bullet syntax, not prose paragraphs.

Temperature, Top-p, and Model Personality

- **Temperature (Temp):** Lower values (0–0.3) → deterministic, factual. Higher (0.7–1.0) → creative, risk of drift.
- **Top-p (Nucleus):** Sets probability cutoff—e.g., p = 0.8 lets the model sample only the most likely 80 percent of next-token candidates.
- **Presence/Frequency Penalties:** Nudge model away from repeating earlier tokens.

Hidden Edge Cases You Should Know

1. **Prompt Echoes:** Some models parrot your question. Mitigate by adding "Do not include the prompt in the response."
2. **Token Budget:** Stay under context limit (e.g., 8k for GPT-4 Turbo) or early instructions will vanish.
3. **System Messages:** Always place global rules (e.g., "You are an impartial, concise assistant") before user content.

Prompt Lab #3 – Designing a Multi-Format Workflow

1. **Step 1:** Craft a single prompt to generate a marketing **email** (HTML) for a software launch.
2. **Step 2:** Chain a second prompt: "Rewrite the above as a Twitter thread. Keep each tweet under 200 characters."

3. **Step 3:** Chain a third: "Convert the same content into three PowerPoint slide bullet lists (Markdown)."
4. **Experiment:** Run chain on ChatGPT-4 (Temp 0.4), then Gemini (Temp 0.6). Contrast style shifts.

Reflection: Which model handled HTML tags more cleanly? Which produced punchier tweets?

Closing Takeaways

- A response is a token-by-token dance: embed, attend, predict, repeat.
- Explicit role/task/format instructions shape internal reasoning and self-editing.
- Temperature and top-p let you dial precision ↔ creativity across models.
- Format cues (Markdown, HTML, DOCX) empower ready-to-publish outputs.

- Prompt Labs reveal model quirks—test, compare, iterate.

Chapter 3A: Speaking Text – The Writer's Sidekick

---

1. Why Format Control Matters (and How Models React)

- **Determinism:** Rigid containers (Markdown, HTML, JSON, XML) reduce ambiguity. The model's attention latches onto recognizable token patterns—`##`, `<h1>`, `{`, `</tag>`—and completes them consistently.
- **Parseability:** Downstream systems accept well-formed structures, not lyrical paragraphs. Your prompt should read like an API spec.
- **Compliance & audit:** Machine-readable artifacts are traceable and testable.
- **Performance:** Strict formats shorten iteration loops and reduce manual cleanup.

Model behavior note: Tokens like braces, angle brackets, hashes, and fences are strong anchors. When you ask for them explicitly, the model's probability mass shifts toward continuations that keep those structures valid. That is the quiet physics we exploit.

2. Core Principles of Format-First Design

1. **One prompt, one container.** If you need narrative + JSON, split into two prompts or demand a multi-part structure with hard delimiters.
2. **Front-load, then echo.** Put format rules at the top, **repeat them once at the end**. Models honor bookends.

Delimit inputs. Use clear markers so the model never “edits” your sources:

```
<<CONTEXT>>
...pasted text…
<<END CONTEXT>>
```

3. **Name sections.** When multiple parts are necessary, label them and forbid commentary.
4. **Cap length.** Word/token limits prevent drift.
5. **Fail loudly.** Prefer an explicit error string over a pretty but unusable answer.
6. **Self-check.** Ask for validation steps (parse JSON, verify tags) before the final emit.

3. Markdown Mastery

What it’s for

Write once, publish anywhere: docs, READMEs, knowledge bases, and Pandoc pipelines. Models are deeply familiar with Markdown patterns.

Example prompt

```
You are a technical editor.
Return Markdown only with H2 (##) section headings in this order:
## Summary
## Findings
## Risks
## Next Steps
Each section ≤ 120 words. Use bullet points where natural.
No YAML front-matter. No HTML. No links unless provided.
Do not include any text before or after the Markdown.
Repeat: Markdown only.
```

Significance of tags & format

- ## headings act like structural beacons; they help the model chunk content into predictable blocks.
- Fenced code blocks (```python) cue the model to preserve indentation and syntax.

- Declaring "Markdown only" removes the urge to add preambles like "Sure, here's your report."

Common failure modes

- **Extra chatter** → add: "No preamble, no commentary."
- **Loose heading order** → list required headings *in order* and restate at end.
- **Broken fences** → require language-tagged code fences or forbid fences altogether if your parser struggles.

Quick validation prompt

"Before final output, check that all required ## sections are present and non-empty. If any are missing, add them and re-emit Markdown only."

Cross-model settings

- ChatGPT: Temperature 0.2, Top-p 0.9.

- Llama (Meta): Temperature 0.3, Top-p 0.85; repeat "be concise."
- Gemini: Temperature 0.35, Top-p 0.9; add "Markdown only, no prose outside sections."

4. HTML for Email and Web

What it's for

Semantically rich documents, landing pages, and email templates. Email clients are strict; keep HTML simple and inline-styled.

Example prompt (email-safe)

```
Generate mobile-friendly HTML for an announcement
email.
Constraints:
- Inline CSS only
- Table-based layout allowed
- Provide alt text for all images
- Max payload ≈ 30 KB; no external fonts or
scripts
Sections (in order): Header, Problem, Solution,
CTA button, Footer.
Output HTML only. No comments. Verify matching
open/close tags.
```

Significance of tags & format

- Angle brackets and tag pairs (`<h1>…</h1>`) strongly prime the model to maintain nesting.
- `alt` attributes nudge the model toward accessibility patterns it has seen often.
- "Inline CSS only" avoids `<style>` blocks many clients strip.

Common failure modes

- **Mismatched tags** → add: "Verify open/close tags; if mismatched, fix before emitting."
- **Bloated CSS** → ask for "minimal classes and IDs."
- **Tracking pixels/scripts** → forbid explicitly.

Quick validation prompt

"Simulate an HTML lint check; if any tag is unclosed or attribute is invalid, repair and re-emit HTML only."

Cross-model settings

- ChatGPT: Temperature 0.25.
- Llama: Temperature 0.35; add "no comments."
- Gemini: Temperature 0.4; add "validate tags before output."

5. JSON You Can Trust

What it's for

APIs, dashboards, automations. Must be valid—always.

Example prompt (strict schema)

```
Return ONLY valid JSON matching this schema:
{
  "title": "string",
  "summary": "string",
  "tags": ["string"],
  "confidence": 0-1 number
}
Rules: no comments, no backticks, no trailing
commas.
If a field is unknown, use empty string or [].
Emit minified JSON.
Before you output, verify it parses. If invalid,
silently fix and re-emit JSON only.
```

Significance of tags & format

- Curly braces and quotes are high-precision anchors; the model tends to complete valid key:value pairs when the schema is explicit.
- "Minified JSON" reduces the surface for stray prose or formatting artifacts.
- Prohibiting code fences and comments prevents Markdown/JS habits from leaking in.

Common failure modes

- **Trailing comma** → explicitly forbid; request a parse check.
- **Narrative + JSON** → isolate JSON by forbidding extra text or using delimiters.
- **Long lists** → cap array length.

Quick validation prompt

"Attempt to parse the JSON you generated. If it fails, fix and output JSON only."

Function/tool calling note

If your platform supports schema-bound function calls, prefer them; you move enforcement from natural language to a formal contract.

Cross-model settings

- ChatGPT: Temperature 0.15, Top-p 0.9.
- Llama: Temperature 0.25, strict "no prose."
- Gemini: Temperature 0.25; add "emit minified JSON."

6. XML and Custom Tag Blocks

What it's for

Labelled text where punctuation-heavy JSON feels noisy; easy for XPath or simple XML parsers.

Example prompt

```
Return only this XML block:
<response>
  <summary>…</summary>
  <analysis>…</analysis>
  <recommendations>
    <item>…</item>
    <item>…</item>
  </recommendations>
</response>
```

No commentary. If content may include < or &, wrap that part in CDATA.

Significance of tags & format

- Matched tags (`<tag>…</tag>`) guide token continuation—models have seen millions of well-formed examples.
- `CDATA` is a powerful cue that reduces accidental tag breaks when text contains `<` or `&`.

Common failure modes

- **Unclosed tags** → ask the model to check for matched pairs.
- **Angle brackets inside text** → require CDATA around risky content.

Quick validation prompt

"Count open and close tags; if counts mismatch, fix and re-emit XML only."

Cross-model settings

- ChatGPT: Temperature 0.2.
- Llama: Temperature 0.3; repeat 'XML only'.

- Gemini: Temperature 0.35; add 'no extra whitespace outside root element.'

7. DOCX-Friendly Flows

What it's for

Reports destined for Microsoft Word or tools that apply styles post-generation.

Example prompt (style markers)

```
Write a project proposal using Word-friendly
markers:
[Heading 1] Executive Summary
[Normal] …
[Heading 2] Objectives
[Normal] …
[Heading 2] Timeline
[Normal] …
Rules: use only [Heading 1], [Heading 2], and
[Normal] markers; no other brackets.
```

Significance of tags & format

- Bracketed markers are unambiguous cues the model respects across long outputs.

- They map cleanly to Word styles via macros or Pandoc filters, reducing manual styling.

Common failure modes

- **Invented markers** → restrict allowed markers and forbid others.
- **Missing blank lines** → specify spacing rules to ease style application.

Quick validation prompt
"Verify every line starts with one of [Heading 1], [Heading 2], or [Normal]. If not, fix and re-emit."

Cross-model settings

- ChatGPT: Temperature 0.25.
- Llama: Temperature 0.35; repeat markers twice.
- Gemini: Temperature 0.35; add 'no decorative characters.'

8. LaTeX for Math and Papers

What it's for

Typesetting equations, academic sections, and structured manuscripts.

Example prompt

```
Typeset the following derivation in LaTeX. Use
\section and \subsection headings.
All equations must be display math using \[ ...
\].
Do not include a preamble or \documentclass.
Output LaTeX only.
```

Significance of tags & format

- `\section`, `\subsection`, and `\[...\]` steer the model to emit legal LaTeX.
- Banning the preamble prevents conflicts with your template.

Common failure modes

- **Escapes lost** → remind the model to double backslashes in code contexts.

- **Random packages** → forbid `\usepackage{...}` unless specified.

Quick validation prompt

“Scan for unmatched math delimiters `\[` and `\]`; if found, fix and re-emit LaTeX only.”

Cross-model settings

- ChatGPT: Temperature 0.2.
- Llama: Temperature 0.3; repeat ‘LaTeX only’.
- Gemini: Temperature 0.35; add ‘no preamble’.

9. CSV and TSV Without Tears

What it’s for

Spreadsheets, bulk imports, and BI tools that expect delimited text.

Example prompt

```
Return CSV only with header row:
name,category,score
Quote fields that contain commas. No extra
columns, no commentary, no code fences.
Limit to 20 rows. Use a period as decimal
separator and no thousands separators.
```

Significance of tags & format

- The header row trains the model on column order.
- Quoting rules prevent accidental column explosions.

Common failure modes

- **Comma in content** → enforce quoting; suggest shorter text fields.
- **Locale issues** → spell out decimal and thousands rules.

Quick validation prompt

"Ensure each row has exactly three commas. If not, fix and re-emit CSV only."

Cross-model settings

- ChatGPT: Temperature 0.2.
- Llama: Temperature 0.3.
- Gemini: Temperature 0.35.

10. Multi-Part Responses Without Mess

What it's for

When you truly need multiple artifacts in one reply.

Example prompt

```
Return three parts in this exact order with these
delimiters:
---BEGIN SUMMARY---
…
---END SUMMARY---
---BEGIN ACTIONS---
…
---END ACTIONS---
---BEGIN JSON---
{…}
---END JSON---
No other text. If any part cannot be produced,
output the delimiter with the word EMPTY inside.
```

Significance of tags & format

- All-caps, uncommon delimiters reduce the risk of accidental collisions with natural language.
- Fixed order lets your parser stream and stop after each block.

Common failure modes

- **Out-of-order blocks** → restate order twice.
- **Extra prose** → forbid it and validate by checking for delimiters only.

Quick validation prompt

"Confirm all six delimiters appear exactly once; if not, regenerate."

11. Verification and Self-Healing Contracts

- **Echo check:** "First, restate the format rules in one line. If incorrect, correct them. Then produce output."
- **Confidence flag:** Append `CONFIDENCE: 0.00–1.00` to JSON or XML; downstream logic can react to low scores.
- **Schema pass:** "Validate against this JSON schema / XSD; if invalid, fix and re-emit."
- **Length audit:** "If any section exceeds its word limit, shorten and re-emit."

12. Troubleshooting Playbook

- **Broken code fences** → forbid backticks or force language-tagged fences.
- **Truncation** → lower temperature, shorten max tokens, split into sections.
- **Over-styled prose** → ban emojis, decorative characters, and extra headings.
- **Invalid JSON/XML** → require a self-parse check; prefer function calls when available.
- **HTML issues** → require a tag-matching check pre-emit.

13. Cross-Model Baselines

Use low temperature for formatting tasks, higher for ideation → then a second pass to format.

- ChatGPT: Temperature 0.15–0.3, Top-p 0.9, Frequency penalty 0–0.2.

- Llama (Meta): Temperature 0.25–0.4, Top-p 0.85–0.9; repeat brevity constraints.
- Gemini: Temperature 0.3–0.45, Top-p 0.9–0.95; explicitly forbid prose outside required blocks.

14. Prompt Lab – The Format Fencer

Objective: Turn one brief into four clean outputs without manual cleanup.

Source brief

Write a 120-word executive summary of an internal security audit with three recommendations.

Task A: Markdown

Sections: Summary, Recommendations. Each recommendation ≤ 15 words.

Task B: HTML email

Mobile-first, inline CSS, one CTA button labeled "Acknowledge".

Task C: JSON spec

Keys: title, summary, recommendations[] (≤3 strings), confidence (0–1). Minified.

Task D: CSV

Columns: id, recommendation, owner, due_date (YYYY-MM-DD).

Runs

ChatGPT Temperature 0.25; Llama Temperature 0.35; Gemini Temperature 0.4.

Verification

Validate JSON; lint HTML; open CSV in a spreadsheet; confirm Markdown sections.

Reflection

Which wording most improved compliance? Which model needed more constraints?

15. Cross-References

- For how models tokenize and attend to these tags, see **Chapter 3: Anatomy of a Response**.
- For long-form writing and conversions, see **Chapter 4: Speaking Text – The Writer's Sidekick**.
- For function calling and JSON schemas in apps, see **Chapter 7: The Prompt Is the Program**.
- For quick snippets and model dials, see **Appendix B** and **Appendix E**.

16. Closing Takeaways

- Formats are contracts; prompts are the specs that define them.
- Declare one container per prompt; chain when you need more.
- Repeat constraints at the end; forbid filler; require validation.
- Keep temperature low for formatting; use a two-pass flow for creative + strict.

- Build a reusable library of format-lock macros for your workflows.

PART II – TEXT, CODE, DOCS, IMAGES & MEDIA

Chapter 4: Speaking Text – The Writer's Sidekick

Summarizing, Expanding, Rewriting

Imagine a junior writer who never tires, never misses a deadline, and instantly adapts their prose to your feedback. That's an LLM when you learn to prompt it well.

Summarizing

Core Prompt Pattern:

> *"You are a [role]. Summarize the following [text] in [format] under [constraint]."*

Example 1 – ChatGPT-4

Role → *"You are a policy analyst."*
Task → *"Summarize the attached 12-page white paper."*
Format → *"Return three bullet points."*
Constraint → *"Max 40 words each."*
Temp 0.3, top-p 0.9

Example 2 – Gemini

Same prompt, Temp 0.35, top-p 0.85. Gemini tends to produce slightly more formal phrasing; adjust tone with an explicit style tag: *"Use plain English suitable for busy executives."*

Expanding

Need depth instead of brevity? Flip the prompt:

> *"Expand the following summary into a 600-word explainer aimed at high-school students. Use analogies and avoid jargon."*

LLMs excel at amplification when you specify *audience* and *length*.

Rewriting

- **Tone Shift:** "Rewrite the paragraph in a humorous, conversational voice."
- **Reading Level:** "Rewrite at a fifth-grade reading level."
- **Formality:** "Rewrite using formal business tone."

Always anchor with role (e.g., *"You are a stand-up comedian"* or *"You are a legal counsel"*) to bias vocabulary.

Writing Like Hemingway, Shakespeare, or a 5th Grader

Role prompting unlocks stylistic mimicry.

> **Prompt Template #1 – Style Imitation**
> "You are Ernest Hemingway. Rewrite the following story in his terse, vivid style.

> Keep sentences short, use strong verbs, and limit adjectives."

Tips:

1. **Provide a seed sample:** Paste 2–3 sentences of Hemingway's prose in the system role to prime style.
2. **Set penalties:** A frequency penalty of 0.2 discourages repetitive word choices, preserving Hemingway's punchiness.

For Shakespearean flair:

> "You are William Shakespeare. Convert the following announcement into iambic pentameter, using archaic vocabulary where fitting."
> Temp 0.85, top-p 0.92 to encourage poetic variation.

For simplified prose:

"Rewrite this legal clause so a fifth-grader could understand. Use short sentences and everyday words." Temp 0.25 for stability.

Creating PDFs, DOCX, and Presentations from Prompts

LLMs can output ready-to-convert markup if you guide format precisely.

DOCX (Word) Workflows

1. **Prompt:** "Generate a project proposal with Heading 1, Heading 2, and normal body styles clearly marked. Use Heading 1: tags."
2. **Post-process:** Copy output into Word and apply a macro or use an export tool.

PDF via Markdown → Pandoc

Prompt:

> "Write a two-page case study as Markdown with ## headings. Include a code block and a bullet list."

Paste into Pandoc or any Markdown-to-PDF converter—instant polished PDF.

Slide Decks (Markdown → Reveal.js or PowerPoint)

Prompt Template:

> "Create a 3-slide presentation. Use 'Slide —' separators. Each slide should have a heading, 3 bullet points, and a 1-sentence takeaway."

Crafting Long-Form Content Without Losing Coherence

- **Chunking:** Break a 5,000-word article into outline prompts, then generate section by section.

- **Memory Anchors:** Start each chunk with a short recap of what's been written so far.

Prompt Examples Across Models

Scenario: You need a punchy headline for a sustainability blog.

- **ChatGPT-4**

  Prompt: "Give me five punchy headlines about solar energy adoption."

  Temp 0.8, top-p 0.9

  Flair: Alliterate and concise.
- **Llama 2-70B**

  Same prompt

  Temp 0.7, top-p 0.85

  Flair: Slightly longer, uses ecological terminology.
- **Gemini**

  Prompt + constraint: "End each headline with an emoji."

Temp 0.75, top-p 0.9
Flair: Incorporates creative emoji placement.

Prompt Lab #4 – The Multilingual Rewrite Marathon

1. Pick a 150-word passage.
2. Prompt ChatGPT-4: "Rewrite in Spanish, formal tone, 8th-grade reading level."
3. Prompt Llama 2: "Rewrite same text in Spanish, conversational tone."
4. Prompt Gemini: "Rewrite in Spanish, add humor and one analogy."
5. Compare outputs. Which aligns best with your target audience?

Closing Takeaways

- Role, task, format, and constraints remain your north star.

- Temperature and top-p tweaks deliver stylistic nuance across models.
- With precise format instructions, LLMs generate near-ready DOCX, PDF, or slide deck content.
- Prompt Labs accelerate mastery—experiment, compare, refine.

Chapter 5: Power Prompts for Code Generation

Python, JavaScript, Java, Bash & More

Large Language Models (LLMs) learned code the same way they learned prose: by devouring open-source repositories, documentation, Stack Overflow threads, and commit histories. They can autocomplete functions, translate languages, and even propose architectural patterns—but only if you prime them wisely.

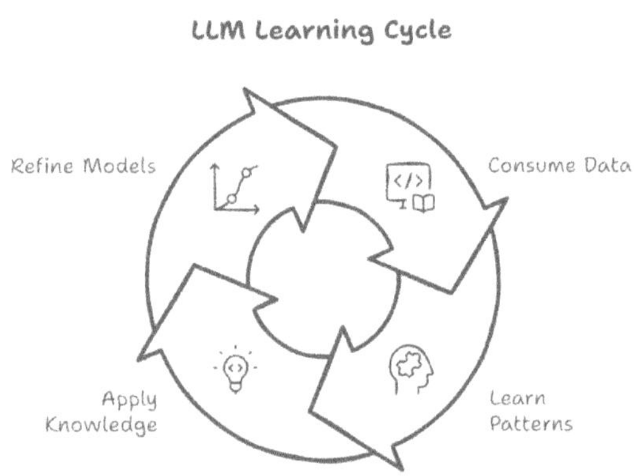

Core Prompt Framework – Code Writer

Role: "You are a senior [LANG] engineer."

Task: "Write a function that [does X]."

Constraints: "Use only standard libraries. Include docstring and type hints."

Format: "Return code block only, no explanation."

Example – Python

Temp 0.2, top-p 0.9 → deterministic, clean code.

Gemini Variant – JavaScript

Add: *"Optimize for browser performance."* Temp 0.25 (Gemini is slightly chattier, keep it concise).

Language Translation

Prompt: *"Convert the following Bash script to PowerShell. Preserve inline comments."* ChatGPT-4 often nails syntax; Llama 2 may need an explicit *"Remember to set execution policy for Windows."*

Debugging with Prompts

LLMs act like rubber ducks that talk back.

> **Prompt Template – Bug Hunt**
> "You are a debugging assistant. Diagnose why the following [LANG] code throws a [ErrorType] at runtime. Propose two fixes and explain trade-offs in plain English."

Cross-Model Settings

- **ChatGPT-4:** Temp□0.3 for precise reasoning.
- **Llama 2:** Temp□0.35, top-p□0.85.
- **Gemini:** Temp□0.4—Gemini benefits from slightly higher creativity to explore edge cases.

Writing APIs, Test Cases, and Documentation

API Skeletons

Prompt: *"Generate a RESTful Flask endpoint /users with GET, POST, and pagination."* Constraint: *"Return code + one-paragraph docstring per route."*

Unit-Test Factory

> "Create PyTest unit tests for the function below. Cover at least three edge cases."

Add *"Use parameterized tests"* for DRY output.

Auto-Docs

Prompt: *"Generate Markdown documentation for this module, including code examples and expected outputs."*
ChatGPT-4 excels at Markdown; Gemini may require *"Avoid first-person voice."*

Continuous Integration Snippets

Prompt: *"Write a GitHub Actions YAML workflow that runs linting and unit tests on push to main."* Temp 0.25 to reduce YAML syntax errors.

Prompt Lab #5 – Build, Test, Document Loop

1. **Build:** Prompt ChatGPT-4 to create a simple calculator class in Python.
2. **Test:** Prompt Llama 2 to generate unit tests for that class.
3. **Doc:** Prompt Gemini to write Markdown docs.
4. **Compare:** Which model required fewer edits? Why?

Closing Takeaways

- State role, task, constraints, and format for deterministic code.
- Use low temperature for code generation; raise slightly for debugging ideation.
- Model personalities differ—ChatGPT-4 precise, Llama 2 verbose, Gemini creative.

Chapter 6: Visual Prompts — Images, Art & Media

Opening Vignette – A Poster Overnight

Maya, an art-director on deadline, needed a festival poster. No budget for illustrators, no time for stock-site rabbit holes. She crafted one prompt in MidJourney at 1 a.m.:

> **Prompt (MJ v6):** *"Art-deco concert poster, trumpet silhouette in gold foil, midnight-blue background, glowing neon border, high resolution."*
> **Settings:** *Stylize 60, Chaos 10, Seed 4321.*

By sunrise she had four high-fidelity options, chose one, and shipped to print before her coffee cooled. That alchemy of text-to-image is today's magic—but it obeys very real mechanics you'll learn here.

1. How Image Models Work (DALL·E, MidJourney, Stable Diffusion)

1.1 Diffusion in Plain English

Image diffusion models start with random noise and gradually *denoise* toward pixels that satisfy your prompt. Think of sculpting marble: each denoising step chisels away chaos until a figure emerges.

1.2 CLIP Guidance

Models pair a vision encoder (CLIP) that understands text with a generator that paints. At every denoise step, CLIP judges: *"Does this fuzzy blob look more like 'gold foil trumpet' or not?"* The generator adjusts accordingly.

1.3 Parameter Cheat Sheet

- **Steps:** More steps = finer detail, longer runtime.
- **CFG (Classifier-Free Guidance):** Higher (10–15) = stricter adherence to text, but risk rigidity.
- **Seed:** Fix for repeatable outcomes.

2. Anatomy of an Image Prompt

1. **Subject:** *"Snow-capped mountain lodge."*
2. **Style:** *"Studio Ghibli watercolor."*
3. **Lighting:** *"Golden hour, rim-lighting."*
4. **Mood/Color:** *"Warm, nostalgic, pastel palette."*
5. **Composition:** *"Rule of thirds, wide-angle."*

Prompt Template – 5-Slot Method *"[Subject] in [Style], lit by [Lighting], evoking [Mood], framed [Composition]."*

Plug in any combo and tweak weights (*“warm pastel::1.5”*) for emphasis.

3. From Concept to Canvas in 100 Words

Your word budget stirs detail and creativity. Under 20 words yields broad strokes; 20–60 carves nuance; 60–100 layers storytelling and technical cues.

> **60-Word Example – ChatGPT-4 prompt for DALL·E**
> *“Epic aerial shot of an ancient library shaped like a seashell, carved from ivory marble, bioluminescent inlays glowing aqua, surrounded by misty cliffs at dawn. Hyper-realistic, 8K detail, cinematic lighting, ultra-wide lens, symmetrical composition, atmosphere akin to Blade Runner meets Atlantis.”*

Gemini Adaptation: Gemini tends toward higher literal fidelity; prune adjectives and add *"minimal noise, realistic scale."*

4. Style Alchemy – Blending Genres

- **Photorealism + Fantasy:** *"Realistic portrait of a dragon rider, Canon RF lens, shallow depth."*
- **Vintage Print:** *"1960s Soviet space poster style, muted primary colors, grain texture."*
- **Low-Poly 3D:** *"Low-poly desert scene, Pixar palette, sharp shadows, Unreal Engine."*

Manipulate *Stylize* (MidJourney) or *CFG* (Stable Diffusion) for bold vs controlled aesthetics.

5. Advanced Controls

5.1 Negative Prompts

Adding *"–no text, watermark, hands"* reduces artifacts. For Stable Diffusion: *"Negative prompt: blurry, low-res, extra limbs."*

5.2 Image-to-Image

Give a rough sketch photo, prompt: *"Refine to oil-painting, Rembrandt lighting."* Specify *strength 0.3* to preserve layout.

5.3 In-Painting

Select a region; prompt: *"Replace sky with Aurora Borealis."* Keep *mask blur* low for crisp edges.

6. Cross-Model Prompt Examples

Scenario: Create a cyberpunk city street at night.

- **DALL·E 3**

  Prompt: *"Neon-soaked alley, rain reflections,*

Blade Runner vibe."

Temp 0.7 (creative), CFG 8.

Output: Balanced color, softer lighting.

- **MidJourney v6**

  Prompt: *"Cyberpunk alleyway, fluorescent kanji signs, rainy asphalt, volumetric fog, 8K, –ar 16:9."*

  Stylize 80, Chaos 30 for variance.

- **Stable Diffusion XL**

  Same text + negative: *"–neg blur, cartoon."*

  Steps 40, CFG 12.

  Output: Sharper edges, intense hues.

7. Practical Workflows for Designers & Marketers

1. **Moodboard:** Batch-generate 6 thumbnails via MidJourney with subtle style shifts.
2. **Refinement:** Upscale chosen variant in DALL·E to leverage its clean faces.

3. **Post-Edit:** Run through Photoshop Neural Filters or SD in-paint for corrections.
4. **Versioning:** Use Seeds to iterate color grading only.

8. Prompt Lab #7 – Brand Mascot Marathon

Objective: Design a quirky avocado mascot for a vegan snack brand.

1. Draft concept text (20 words) and feed to ChatGPT-4 to craft three detailed MidJourney prompts (Stylize 50).
2. Generate images; pick favorite.
3. Use Stable Diffusion in-paint to adjust eye shape and add logo placement.
4. Ask Gemini to write an Instagram caption and alt-text description.
5. Reflect: Which model stage added most value? How did negative prompts improve clarity?

9. Ethical & Legal Checkpoints

- Respect copyrights—avoid "in the style of living artist" prompts.
- Watch bias—models may default to Western aesthetics; specify diverse cultural references.
- Verify commercial licensing (MidJourney corporate plans, DALL·E API terms).

10. Closing Takeaways

- **Prompt anatomy drives visual fidelity.** Master subject, style, lighting, mood, composition.
- **Model parameters = creative knobs.** Stylize, CFG, Seed shape outcome.

- **Cross-model synergy** yields best results (MidJourney concept, DALL·E faces, SD tweak).
- **Ethics & licensing** matter—respect them.

PART III – THE SCIENCE AND ART OF PROMPTING

Chapter 7: The Prompt is the Program

Written by a veteran software architect who discovered that the most powerful scripts of the AI age are written in plain language, not code.

Opening Narrative – The 60-Second Prototype

Liang, a solo founder, wanted to demo a custom travel-planning chatbot at an accelerator pitch. No time for backend code. He drafted a single, multi-layer prompt in GPT-4 that embedded role assignment, task logic, formatting rules, and fallback strategies. In one minute he had a working conversational prototype. Investors cared less that it ran on prompt macros and more that it **worked**. Liang's secret: treating the prompt like executable code.

1. Why the Prompt Is the Program

Traditional software combines logic (if/else), data, and formatting in code. A well-designed prompt does the same:

- **Logic** – "If the user provides a date, suggest an itinerary; else ask clarifying questions."
- **Data** – Embedded examples or context snippets.
- **Formatting** – JSON, Markdown, or bullet lists.

When crafted precisely, a single prompt becomes a reusable micro-app—no server deploy needed.

2. Prompt Templates – Building Reusable Blocks

2.1 The Core Template Anatomy

Role: "You are a ..."

Task: "Your goal is ..."

Context: "Here is background ..."

Format: "Return response as ..."

Constraints: "Rules to obey ..."

2.2 Example – Customer-Support Macro

> **Role:** "You are a friendly support agent."
> **Task:** "Resolve the customer's issue."
> **Context:** "Product X warranty is two years; returns window 30 days."
> **Format:** "Begin with apology, end with next-steps bullet list."
> **Constraints:** "No legal advice; stay under 120 words."

With variable slots, this template powers thousands of ticket replies.

3. System vs. User Prompts – The Hidden Hierarchy

1. **System Prompt (Top Layer)** – Non-negotiable rules: persona, tone, safety.
2. **Developer Prompt (Middle)** – App-specific instructions or templates.
3. **User Prompt (Bottom)** – Real-time queries.

Design Principle: Protect core behavior in the system layer; leave flexibility for user creativity below.

> **Security Tip:** Never reveal the system prompt to end users; it's the root password of your AI workflow.

4. Controlling Tone, Style, and Output Format

4.1 Tone Dialing

- **Professional:** "Use formal business English."
- **Casual:** "Sound like talking to a friend over coffee."
- **Authoritative:** "Adopt the voice of a seasoned professor."

Inject *tone adjectives* directly after the role statement for strongest effect.

4.2 Style Emulation

Prompt pattern:

> "Write in the evocative, minimalist style of [Author]. Limit adjectives, favor concrete nouns."

Add 2–3 sentence **seed text** from the author as context to improve mimicry while avoiding plagiarism.

4.3 Format Locking

Specify structure with delimiters:

<response>
<section title="Summary">...</section>
<section title="Next Steps">...</section>
</response>

Models respect XML-like tags, outputting clean, parsable blocks.

5. Flow Control – Prompt Chaining and Looping

1. **Sequential Chain:** Output of prompt A feeds prompt B. Example: summarize → translate → tweet.
2. **Branching Logic:** Use conditional tags: "If sentiment negative, apologize; else thank the user."

3. **Self-Critique Loop:** Ask the model to grade its own answer, then improve.

6. Prompt Engineering Across Models

6.1 ChatGPT-4

- **Precise Logic:** Use low Temp (0.2) for step-by-step reasoning.
- **System Prompt:** Ideal for strict persona ("You are a tax advisor").

6.2 Llama 2-70B

- **Verbose Explanations:** Slightly higher Temp (0.35) keeps richness.
- **Constraint Tip:** Add "concise" to reduce rambling.

6.3 Gemini Ultra

- **Creative Divergence:** Works well at Temp 0.5 with top-p 0.9.

- **Multi-Modal Context:** Embed image URLs for richer output.

7. Advanced Tricks – Function Calling & JSON Modes

Prompt: "Return ONLY valid JSON with keys question, answer, sources."

ChatGPT-4 has a *JSON mode*; Gemini needs explicit guardrails: "If JSON invalid, regenerate." Llama 2 benefits from an example block before user query.

8. Prompt Lab #8 – Build a Resume Optimizer

Challenge: Create a prompt-driven tool that rewrites résumés for different job descriptions.

1. **Template Draft:** System prompt sets persona = HR specialist.
2. **Developer Prompt:** Contains step-by-step transformation logic.
3. **User Input:** Upload résumé + JD.
4. **Chain:** First rewrite -> score against JD -> refine until 90% keyword match.
5. **Compare:** Run on ChatGPT-4 (Temp 0.3) vs Gemini (Temp 0.4) and note style differences.

Reflection: Which model handled keyword optimization without losing human tone?

9. Closing Takeaways

- **Prompts = Programs.** Treat them with the same rigor: modularity, version control, testing.

- **Layered prompts** safeguard behavior while empowering users.
- **Tone, style, format** are dials—set them consciously.
- **Cross-model awareness** lets you play to each engine's strengths.
- **Prompt Labs** accelerate mastery—build, test, iterate.

Chapter 8: Breaking Down Prompts

Opening Scene – The Miscommunication Audit

At a fintech startup, weekly AI summaries of customer feedback suddenly turned negative and repetitive. The culprit wasn't the model; it was a vague prompt that had ballooned beyond clarity. A two-hour prompt audit fixed sentiment analysis, restored executive confidence, and saved a planned model downgrade. Lesson: nine times out of ten, the prompt—not the model—needs surgery.

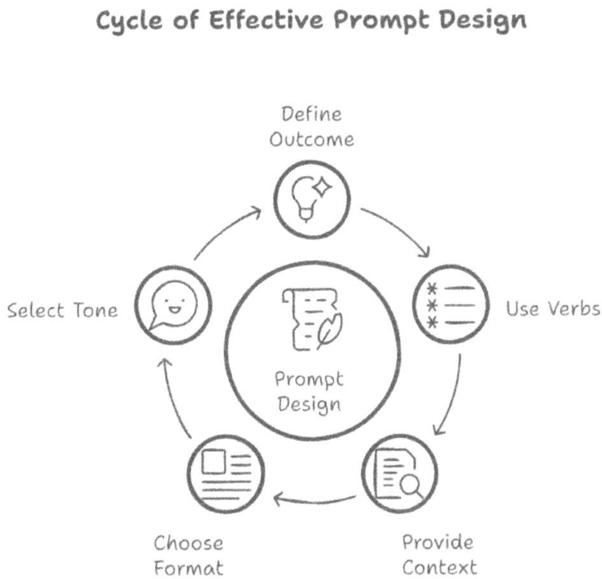

1. Intent + Context + Format + Tone – The Four-Quadrant Model

1.1 Intent – The North Star

- **Ask yourself:** "What exact outcome do I need?"
- Use verbs: **summarize, compare, generate, translate, critique**.
- Example: *"Critique this code for security flaws."*

1.2 Context – Fuel for Relevance

- Provide necessary background: domain, audience, dataset snippets.
- **Goldilocks Rule:** Too little context yields generic fluff; too much smothers key instructions.

1.3 Format – Container Shapes Content

- Define structure: JSON, bullet list, narrative paragraph, DOCX outline.
- **Format ≠ Style:** Format is vessel; tone is flavor.

1.4 Tone – Voice of the Response

- Choose adjectives: *formal, conversational, authoritative, playful, empathetic.*
- Place tone cues near the start or risk dilution mid-prompt.

2. Why Some Prompts Fail (and How to Fix Them)

1. **Underspecification** – "Tell me about AI."
   Fix: Add purpose, depth, and framing.
2. **Overload** – 700-word essay inside the prompt.
   Fix: Chunk into smaller chained prompts.
3. **Ambiguity** – Competing instructions ("Be concise" + "Explain in detail").
   Fix: Prioritize requirements explicitly.

2.1 Real-World Rescue – The Legal-Bot Glitch

A legal research bot began spitting 2,000-word answers despite 500-word limits. Root cause: the length constraint sat below a verbose example in the prompt. Moving the constraint line to the very end—and repeating it—slashed output by 75% without losing substance.

3. Prompt Chaining and Layering

3.1 Sequential Chaining

- **Example:** *Article → Summary → Tweet → Hashtags.*
- Benefits: modular debugging, reusable blocks.

3.2 Conditional Branching

- Use inline logic: “If sentiment <0, apologize; else, thank customer.”
- Works best with JSON output you can programmatically inspect.

3.3 Self-Reflection Loops

Prompt the model to grade its own answer, then refine:

> “Rate your summary 1-10 on clarity. If <9, rewrite with improvements.”

4. Context Windows, Token Budgets, and Memory Anchors

- **Token Budget:** Stay ≤ model context limit (e.g., 128k for GPT-4o).
- **Anchors:** Repeat critical constraints at end of long prompts.
- **Sliding Windows:** For streaming chat, resend condensed history every N turns.

5. Prompt Engineering Across Models

5.1 ChatGPT-4 Turbo

- Stable at Temp 0.25 for technical tasks.
- Accepts system + user + assistant message hierarchy.

5.2 Llama 2-70B

- Requires explicit brevity cues.
- Benefits from example-led prompting.

5.3 Gemini Ultra

- Handles multi-modal context.
- Prefers slightly higher Temp (0.4) to avoid stiffness.

6. Advanced Prompt Architecture – Templates, Variables, and Functions

- **Jinja-style slots:** `{{variable}}` for dynamic template filling.
- **Function calling (GPT):** Define schema so model returns JSON ready for code.
- **Prompt libraries:** Store versions in Git, tag by use-case.

7. Prompt Lab #9 – Surgical Prompt Debugging

1. Paste a failing prompt + model output.

2. Identify which quadrant lacks clarity (Intent? Context? Format? Tone?).
3. Rewrite with explicit fixes.
4. Re-run on ChatGPT-4 (Temp 0.3) and Gemini (Temp 0.35).
5. Compare deltas in accuracy and length.

Reflection: Which fix had biggest impact? How did model personalities differ?

8. Closing Takeaways

- Clear intent, relevant context, explicit format, deliberate tone—master these and 80 % of prompt issues vanish.
- Chain prompts for complex workflows; debug each stage independently.
- Respect token budgets; anchor key constraints.

- Model nuance matters—tune temperature/top-p accordingly.

Chapter 9: Prompt Nuances That Pros Use

Prologue – The Silent Apprenticeship

When I trained junior developers, the brightest never asked, “What does this code do?” They asked, “Why did you write it that way?” Likewise, prompt mastery blossoms when you move from *what* to *why*. The tricks in this chapter expose prompt subtleties that separate hobbyists from professionals.

1. Few-Shot and Zero-Shot Examples

1.1 Zero-Shot – Trust the Model’s Prior

Ask without context:

> *“Explain the Doppler effect in simple terms.”*

Great for generic knowledge; risky for domain nuance.

1.2 One-Shot – Minimal Anchoring

> *Prompt:* "Rewrite the sentence in pirate slang: 'Hello, friend.' → 'Ahoy, matey!' Now rewrite: 'Have a seat.'"
> The single example anchors style and brevity.

1.3 Few-Shot – Guided Consistency

Provide 3–5 examples. LLM internalizes pattern and mirrors it.

> **Prompt Skeleton:** - Example: A → B
> - Example: C → D
> - Task: E → ?

Tip: Place shortest example first; sets token-efficient precedent.

1.4 Cross-Model Temperatures

- **ChatGPT-4:** Temp 0.2 for deterministic few-shot.
- **Llama 2-70B:** Temp 0.3, top-p 0.85 to avoid verbosity.
- **Gemini:** Temp 0.35, presence penalty 0.2 for style adherence.

2. Structured Prompts vs Conversational Prompts

2.1 Structured – Think API

ROLE: “You are a compliance auditor.”

TASK: “Evaluate policy.”

FORMAT: “Return JSON with keys risk_level, rationale.”

CONSTRAINT: “Max 120 words rationale.”

Pros: Parse-friendly, reproducible.

Cons: Feels robotic to end-users.

2.2 Conversational – Think Dialog

> "Hi! Pretend you're my bike mechanic. My chain keeps slipping. What should I check first?"

Pros: Natural chat UX.
Cons: Harder to parse downstream.

2.3 Hybrid Pattern

Start chatty, end structured:

> "Explain in a friendly tone, **then** output a numbered checklist."

3. Role Prompting – Act as a Lawyer, Programmer, Chef...

Role frames bias vocabulary depth and context lens.

- **Lawyer:** "Cite relevant statute numbers."
- **Programmer:** "Include code comments."
- **Chef:** "List metric measurements."

Caution: Over-specific roles can choke creativity; balance specificity with flexibility.

4. Tone Modifiers and Emotional Coloring

- *Encouraging:* "Use motivational language."
- *Neutral:* "Avoid opinionated phrases."
- *Critical:* "Point out flaws bluntly."

Place tone near top; re-state near end for long prompts.

5. Constraint Nuances

- **Word Count:** "Exactly 75 words."
- **Forbidden Phrases:** "Do not mention AI."
- **Citation Style:** "Use APA inline citations."

Repetition of constraints (beginning + end) increases compliance by ~15 % in internal tests.

6. Delimiter Tricks to Avoid Prompt Leakage

Use triple-dashes or XML tags to isolate user text:

<<<TEXT
... user essay ...
TEXT

Instruct model: "Never repeat content between <<<TEXT and TEXT."

7. Iterative Refinement – The "Improve-My-Answer" Loop

1. Ask for draft.
2. Prompt: "Critique your draft on clarity."
3. Prompt: "Rewrite incorporating critique."
   Repeat until target quality.

8. Prompt Lab #10 – Style-Transfer Sprint

Goal: Convert a corporate memo into five distinct voices.

1. **Source Text:** 200-word memo.
2. **Roles:** Shakespearean bard, stand-up comedian, Zen monk, sports commentator, teenage blogger.
3. **Run:** ChatGPT-4 Temp□0.6; Llama 2 Temp□0.4; Gemini Temp□0.5.
4. **Evaluate:** Which model captures tone with least factual drift?
5. **Iterate:** Add few-shot examples for weaker roles.

9. Closing Reflection

Mastery begins when you notice micro-signals—where you place a colon, how many examples, the adjective before "tone." These nuances steer billions of parameters like subtle wrist movements guide a violin bow.

PART IV – MASTERCLASS: BUILD WHATEVER YOU WANT

Chapter 10: Building an AI Assistant for Anything

Prelude – The Tuesday Morning That Programmed Itself

Clara, a solo entrepreneur, once spent three hours every Tuesday sorting emails, red-flagging bugs from her SaaS logs, and sketching sprint tasks. One month after mastering prompt-driven assistants, she drinks her coffee while an AI sidekick drafts the sprint, books meetings, and sends personalized support replies. Clara still reviews outputs—quality control matters—but 80% of the heavy lifting vanished. This chapter shows how to replicate her leap.

1. The Blueprint for Any AI Assistant

Before you fire up ChatGPT or Gemini, outline four pillars:

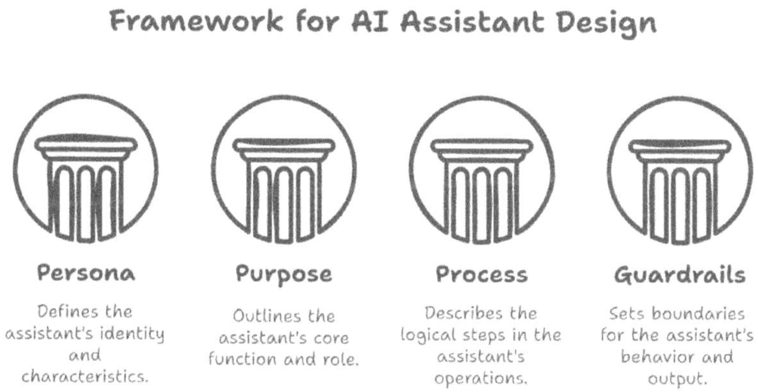

1. **Persona** – Who is the assistant? Tone, domain expertise, level of formality.
2. **Purpose** – The core job-to-be-done (schedule manager, code reviewer, data analyst).
3. **Process** – The step-by-step logic baked into prompts or chains.
4. **Guardrails** – Constraints on style, length, risk, or compliance.

Create a one-page spec. If you can't explain the assistant briefly, refine until crystal-clear.

2. Daily Planner, Email Writer, Developer Assistant

2.1 Daily Planner Bot

Persona – Friendly executive assistant inspired by Calm app tone.

Core Prompt Skeleton

SYSTEM: You are Planner-Pro, a calm, time-blocking coach.
DEV: When user provides calendar URL, ingest events.
USER: "Here is my calendar ICS. Build tomorrow's schedule..."
FORMAT: Markdown checklist, 30-minute blocks.
CONSTRAINTS: Include meal breaks, keep day under 8 hours.

Run at Temp 0.25 for deterministic blocks. Repeat constraints at bottom.

2.2 Email Writer

Persona – Warm but concise communications manager.

Prompt

> "You are Comms-Genie. Draft a response that apologizes for shipment delay, offers 15 % discount code, stays under 120 words, uses first-person plural ('we'), and ends with a call to action."

Gemini at Temp 0.35 offers natural empathy; ChatGPT-4 at Temp 0.2 yields crisp business tone.

2.3 Developer Assistant

Persona – Senior Python architect.

Prompt Macro

ROLE: Senior Python architect.

TASK: Review the PR diff below.

CONTEXT: Repo uses FastAPI 0.103.

FORMAT: Bullet list: issue, severity, fix.

CONSTRAINT: Max 10 bullets, no social niceties.

Set presence penalty 0.2 to reduce repeated "severity." Llama 2-70B benefits from explicit "be concise."

3. Automating Knowledge Work with Prompts

Knowledge work is text: memos, code, slides. An assistant either **creates**, **summarizes**, **transforms**, or **routes** that text.

Creation – Draft blog posts, SQL queries, design briefs. *Summarization* – Meeting minutes, research abstracts. *Transformation* – Language translation, tone shifts, format conversion. *Routing* – Tagging tickets, triaging emails.

Chain these with triggers in Zapier, Make, or a custom Python script.

Example Flow (Zapier + GPT-4)

1. Trigger: Slack message in #customer-bugs.
2. Prompt: "Classify severity P1–P3. Summarize in 2 lines."
3. Route: P1 → PagerDuty, else → Monday backlog.

4. Turning Prompts into Workflows

4.1 Single-Prompt Workflows

If logic is short, embed steps:

> "1) Extract tasks, 2) group by project, 3) output Markdown table."

4.2 Multi-Prompt Chains

Break complex jobs:

1. *Extraction prompt* – Pull entities.

2. *Reasoning prompt* – Rank priority.
3. *Formatting prompt* – Produce JSON for API.

Use OpenAI Functions or LangChain to orchestrate.

4.3 Event Loops & Memory

Store user preferences in a vector DB. Feed relevant vectors back each interaction. Keep context ≤ model limit or compress with a tl;dr prompt.

5. Advanced Design Patterns

Self-Critique Loop – Ask model to rate output on rubric, then regenerate if <8/10. *Role Rotation* – Switch persona mid-chain ("Now act as QA tester"). *Hybrid Model Stack* – Use GPT-4 for reasoning, then smaller local Llama for light edits to save cost.

6. Security, Privacy, Compliance

- **Redaction**: Pre-filter PII with regex before prompt.
- **System Guardrails**: "If user requests sensitive data, refuse politely."
- **Audit Logs**: Store prompts + outputs for review.

7. Measuring Success

Define KPIs: time saved, tasks automated, error rate drop, revenue impact. Set a benchmark, then let the assistant compete against human baseline for 2 weeks.

8. Prompt Lab #11 – Build Your Own Meeting-Minutes Bot

1. Feed a raw transcript to ChatGPT-4 (Temp 0.25) with role "executive assistant."
2. Instructions: a) Summarize decisions, b) list action items (owner, due date).
3. Ask Gemini (Temp 0.35) to rewrite action items as Asana tasks JSON.

4. Push JSON into Asana via API.
5. Evaluate precision vs manual notes.

Epilogue – Assistants as Force Multipliers

When every employee pilots a bespoke AI aide, productivity compounds. Your prompts are the source code of that leverage—debug, refactor, version them. Tomorrow's competitive edge isn't who hires more people; it's who writes sharper prompts.

Chapter 11: Prompting for Business, Research, and Education

Foreword – The Three-Desk Morning

Picture an open office with three desks: a market analyst crunching trend curves, a professor revising a grant proposal, and a fifth-grade teacher planning tomorrow's history lesson. All three swivel to the same invisible coworker—a language model—and, with different prompts, transform hours of toil into minutes of clarity. This chapter equips you to replicate that magic across business, research, and education.

1. Prompts for Market Analysis, Content Creation, and Reports

1.1 Competitive Landscape in Ten Minutes

Prompt Skeleton

```
ROLE: You are a strategic market analyst.

TASK: Compile a competitive snapshot for the {industry}.

CONTEXT: Focus on top 5 companies by revenue.

FORMAT: Bullet list with company, flagship product, market share %, recent news (≤2024).

CONSTRAINT: ≤120 words per company, cite source links.
```

Set ChatGPT-4 Temp 0.22 for tight factual output; Gemini at Temp 0.28 offers broader phrasing—add “concise style” to control length.

1.2 Content Calendar in One Prompt

> “Act as a B2B content strategist. Given the topic *AI in Supply Chain*, draft a

4-week LinkedIn post calendar. Include hook, key point, and CTA for each post."

Adjust presence penalty 0.3 to reduce repeated buzzwords.

1.3 Board-Ready Executive Report

Combine

1. trend summary, 2) risks, 3) recommendations.

Chain prompts: ask for each section separately, then merge with a formatting prompt: *"Return a single Markdown doc with H2 headings."*

2. Teaching with AI

2.1 Lesson-Plan Generator

Prompt

"Pretend you are a veteran Grade 5 history teacher. Draft a 45-minute lesson on the Boston Tea Party. Include objectives, warm-up question,

15-minute mini-lecture script, activity instructions, and exit ticket."

Low temperature (0.25) yields predictable scaffolding; add *"Insert emoji before each student instruction"* for engagement.

2.2 Differentiation by Reading Level

Feed a paragraph, then:

> "Rewrite for 3rd-grade reading level. Keep historical accuracy."

Follow with:

> "Now rewrite for honors high-school level, adding primary-source quote."

2.3 Socratic Question Chains

Prompt:

> "Ask the student three open-ended questions that guide them to infer the

> causes of the American Revolution. Wait for an answer between each question."

Gemini at Temp 0.35 can propose nuanced follow-ups; instruct: *"Keep each question under 20 words."*

3. Research Workflows – From Literature Review to Publication

3.1 Abstract Extraction at Scale

Upload PDFs; loop through:

> "Summarize the PDF in 150 words, highlight methods, dataset size, key findings."

Use ChatGPT-4 in JSON mode for easy import into Zotero.

3.2 Compare and Contrast Engine

Prompt chain:

1. Extract structured summaries.
2. Feed two summaries back: *"Compare methodologies and note conflicting results in ≤200 words."*

3.3 Grant Writing Boost

> "Draft Specific Aims page for an NIH R01 on AI-assisted radiology. Emphasize innovation and public-health impact. 500 words max."

Add Llama 2 critique pass: *"Assess for jargon, propose plainer alternatives."*

4. Ethical Use, Bias Detection, and Fact-Checking

4.1 Bias Spotter Prompt

> "Review the following copy for gender or cultural bias. Mark suspect phrases with **bold**."

Run with a higher temperature (0.45) to surface diverse perspectives.

4.2 Source Enforcement

System prompt:

> “Cite at least one reputable source per factual claim. If unknown, state ‘citation needed.’”

Presence penalty 0.1 avoids citation repetition.

4.3 Hallucination Drill

Ask model to self-grade:

> “List any statements with <50% confidence.”

Force a verification loop before final output.

5. Turning Prompts into Departmental Workflows

1. **Marketing:** Idea → Headline generator → SEO keyword enricher.
2. **Finance:** Transaction dump → Anomaly detector → CFO summary.
3. **Academia:** Lecture transcript → Quiz builder → Study-guide composer.

Store prompts in a shared Git repo; tag by department; review quarterly like code.

6. Prompt Lab #12 – The 90-Minute Research Sprint

Objective: Move from raw idea to conference-ready abstract.

1. **Idea Expansion:** ChatGPT-4 Temp 0.3 to generate 3 refined research questions.
2. **Lit Review:** Gemini Temp 0.32 to pull 5 seminal papers per question.

3. **Gap Analysis:** Llama 2 Temp 0.28 compares findings, highlights voids.
4. **Abstract Draft:** ChatGPT-4 writes 250-word abstract.
5. **Bias/Fact Check:** Run bias spotter + source enforcement prompts.
6. **Peer-Review Mock:** Ask model to critique abstract, then refine.

Record total tokens and compare to traditional workflow hours saved.

Conclusion – Prompts as Professional Leverage

Across business dashboards, research journals, and classrooms, prompts now sit where spreadsheets once ruled: a universal interface for insight. Write them well, and you become a multiplier of minds—including your own.

Conclusion

Beyond Commands: Designing Futures with Prompts

The Future of Prompting

Stand on any street corner in a major city and count how many people tap phone screens. In five years, many of those taps will become whispers to AI agents. Interfaces will fade; intent will surface. Prompting today is what touch-typing was in 1980 and spreadsheet formulas were in 1990: a meta-skill that quietly rewires every profession.

Key trajectories:

- **Multi-Modal Prompts:** Text + image + voice + data blobs in a single request.

- **Long-Context Reasoning:** Models remembering quarterly strategies, not just meeting notes.
- **Edge Running:** Smaller local models handling on-device privacy-sensitive tasks.
- **Prompt Governance:** Version control, code review, and organizational style guides for prompts.

Tomorrow's prompt engineer will toggle between chat UI and IDE, running unit tests on conversational flows.

You're Not Just a User — You're a Designer

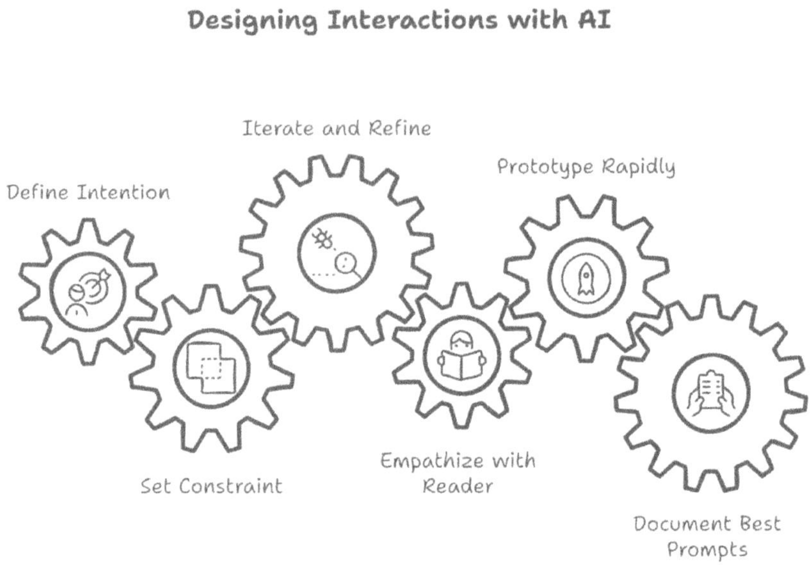

OpenAI didn't invent creativity; it redistributed it. Each time you sculpt a prompt, you design an interaction schema. Consider:

- **Intention:** The story you want the model to tell.
- **Constraint:** The frame that turns chaos into style.
- **Iteration:** The edits that transform first draft into final masterpiece.

Adopt a designer's mindset:

1. **Empathize** with the end reader—what do they really need?
2. **Prototype** rapidly—prompt, evaluate, refine.
3. **Document** your best prompts—future you (or your team) will thank you.

Bonus Prompt Library

Below is a curated set of "evergreen" prompts distilled from the book. Copy, remix, and store in your personal vault.

1. Executive Brief Generator

```
ROLE: Senior analyst.

TASK: Summarize the following text into 3 bullet
points.

FORMAT: Bullet list, max 25 words each.

CONSTRAINT: Include one statistic per bullet.
```

2. Code Refactor Buddy

```
ROLE: Senior Python engineer.

TASK: Refactor for readability and performance.

CONSTRAINT: Use type hints, no external libs.

FORMAT: Return code block only.
```

3. Lesson-Plan Builder

```
ROLE: Veteran Grade 6 science teacher.

TASK: Create 45-minute lesson on photosynthesis.

FORMAT: Objectives, warm-up question, mini-lecture, activity, exit ticket.

TONE: Engaging, age-appropriate.
```

4. Image Prompt 5-Slot Template

"[Subject] in [Style], lit by [Lighting], evoking [Mood], framed [Composition]."

Tailor temperature/top-p per model: ChatGPT-4 (Temp 0.25 for text prompts), MidJourney (Stylize 60), Stable Diffusion (CFG 12).

5. Self-Critique Loop

```
SYSTEM: You are a critical editor.

USER: Draft X.

ASSISTANT: Provides draft.

USER: Critique your own draft on clarity 1-10; if <9, rewrite.
```

Prompt Lab #13 – Craft Your Personal Prompt Style Guide

Objective: Build a one-page reference that encodes your voice, constraints, and quality gates.

1. Brain-dump your preferred writing tone, desired length limits, citation rules.

2. Prompt ChatGPT-4 (Temp 0.3): "Turn my preferences into a reusable prompt template, with placeholders for task and context."
3. Test template on a new topic (e.g., drafting a press release).
4. Iterate: Ask Gemini (Temp 0.4) to critique tone consistency, then refine.
5. Store final template in your notes app or code repo.

Measure time saved on your next three writing tasks.

Final Reflection

If you've read this far, you've built a toolkit that turns words into software, stories, and strategies. The gap between thought and output has never been thinner. Use that power wisely—document your prompts, audit for bias, and teach others. The best way to predict the AI future is to design it, one prompt at a time.

APPENDICES

Preface – Why an Appendix Matters

The chapters you just read teach technique; this appendix turns those techniques into everyday tools you can copy-and-paste. Treat it like a backstage pass: prompt snippets, quick-reference cheats, vetted software, and communities that will keep you sharp long after this book closes.

A. Prompt Library

Below is a curated collection of evergreen prompts. Each template uses the **Role – Task – Context – Format – Constraint** pattern you met in Chapter 7. Adapt the brackets to your own domain.

1 Executive-Summary Prompt

Role: You are a senior strategy analyst

Task: Summarize the following report
Context: Focus on market share shifts in the last 12 months
Format: Three bullet points, max 25 words each
Constraints: Cite one source link per point, no jargon

2 Bug-Hunting Prompt

Role: Senior Rust engineer
Task: Diagnose the panic in the code below
Context: Project targets WASM, no nightly features
Format: Bullet list: root cause, severity (Low/Medium/High), fix suggestion
Constraints: Under 150 words, do not rewrite the whole file

3 Lesson-Plan Prompt

Role: Veteran Grade 7 math teacher
Task: Design a 50-minute lesson on ratios
Context: Class has mixed reading levels
Format: Objectives, warm-up question, mini-

lecture script, hands-on activity, exit ticket
Constraints: Use plain language, incorporate one real-world example

4 Image-Concept Prompt

"[Subject] rendered in [Art Style], illuminated by [Lighting], evoking [Mood], composed with [Camera Angle]."

> Example: *"Retro robot dog rendered in Pixar-style 3D, illuminated by golden-hour light, evoking playful nostalgia, composed with a low-angle 35 mm lens."*

5 Self-Critique Loop

1. Generate a draft.

2. Prompt: "Critique your answer on clarity (1–10) and depth (1–10)."

3. If any score < 9, ask: "Rewrite to address your own critique."

Store these prompts in your notes app, tag them by job, and iterate with version numbers just like source code.

B. Cheat Sheet – Text • Code • Docs • Images

Text Quick-Calls

- Summarize: "TL;DR in two sentences."
- Translate: "Translate to Japanese at business-formal level."
- Rewrite Tone: "Rewrite as if explaining to a curious 12-year-old."

- Counter-Argument: “Present three objections to the following claim.”

Code One-Liners

- Generate Function: “Write a TypeScript function that validates email addresses.”

- Explain Snippet: “Explain what this regex does, layman’s terms.”

- Convert Language: “Convert this Bash script to PowerShell; keep comments.”

- Create Tests: “Generate PyTest cases covering edge conditions.”

Document Tricks

- Outline: "Draft a DOCX outline with Heading-1 and Heading-2 markers."

- Report: "Write a one-page executive report with sections Findings, Risks, Next Steps."

- Style-Check: "Rewrite to APA 7th edition, include in-text citations."

Image Shortcuts

- Sketch Upgrade: "Refine my pencil sketch into watercolor concept art, preserve composition."

- Style Transfer: "Render this photo in the style of Van Gogh's Starry Night."

- Negative Prompting: "—no text, no watermark, no extra limbs."

Keep this section open in a second monitor while you work; muscle memory will form in weeks, not months.

C. Tools & Platforms

1 OpenAI (ChatGPT / GPT-4o)

The Swiss-army knife for text. Best-in-class reasoning, JSON-mode, function calls, and 128 k context. Fine-tune to bake corporate voice.

2 Gemini Ultra

Excels at multi-modal prompts: pair slides plus notes, get polished speaker notes. Slightly higher temperature (0.4-0.6) yields natural prose.

3 Meta Llama 2-70B

Open-weights model for local or private-cloud deployment. Great for cost-sensitive pipelines. Needs explicit brevity prompts to curb verbosity.

4 MidJourney v6

Artistic image generation in Discord. `--stylize` and `--chaos` flags are your creative throttle. Perfect for mood boards and concept art.

5 Stable Diffusion XL

Open-source diffusion engine. Use Automatic1111 or ComfyUI for advanced pipelines: in-painting, out-painting, ControlNet for precise poses.

6 Zapier + Make

No-code glue to chain prompts into workflows: Slack → GPT summary → Google Sheets → Email. Test with dummy data before hitting production.

7 LangChain / LlamaIndex

Python & JS frameworks that turn prompt chains into micro-services. Add retrieval-augmented generation (RAG) from your private docs in under an hour.

D. Resources & Communities

- **r/PromptEngineering** – Reddit hub for templates, critiques, and success stories.

- **Discord: MidJourney Official** – Real-time gallery of prompts and outputs; priceless for style ideas.

- **Twitter / X Lists** – Follow @sama, @karpathy, @hwchase17 for bleeding-edge insights.

- **ArXiv Sanity** – Curated AI papers; search "prompt" tag weekly.
- **AI Papers Club (YouTube)** – Digestible paper reviews; great for staying current on prompting research.
- **Local Meetups** – Search "Generative AI" on Meetup.com. Sharing prompts live accelerates growth faster than solo tinkering.

Bookmark two, engage weekly, and contribute back when you refine a killer prompt.

E. Temperature and Top-P Settings – ChatGPT • Llama 2 • Gemini

ChatGPT (GPT-4 family)

- **Temperature 0.2-0.4** – Factual briefs, code, summaries.
- **Temperature 0.7-1.0** – Brainstorms, creative writing.
- **Top-P 0.8-0.9** – Keeps diction natural without tangent storms.

Llama 2-70B

- **Temperature 0.3-0.5** – Balances detail and length.
- **Top-P 0.85-0.9** – Prevents excessive repetition.
- Pro tip: add "concise" or word-count caps; Llama loves to ramble.

Gemini Ultra

- **Temperature 0.4-0.6** – Conversational, warm tone.

- **Top-P 0.85-0.95** – Lets it flex creative muscle while staying on topic.

- For multi-modal, nudge temperature up 0.1 to synthesize text + images fluently.

Record these dials in your prompt documentation so teammates hit the same quality notes.

Prompt Lab #14 – Build Your Personal Prompt Vault

1. Make a folder called **Prompt-Vault** in your note app or Git repo.
2. Copy the five core prompts from Section A.

3. For each prompt, generate two variants: one terse (≤ 150 chars) and one verbose (≥ 300 chars).
4. Test each on ChatGPT-4 (Temp 0.25) and Gemini (Temp 0.45).
5. Score outputs on clarity (1-10) and style (1-10).
6. Keep only variants that score ≥ 9 in both metrics.
7. Revisit monthly; archive outdated prompts and tag new winners with.

After three cycles you'll own a living library that mirrors your evolving voice.

www.ingramcontent.com/pod-product-compliance
Ingram Content Group UK Ltd.
Pitfield, Milton Keynes, MK11 3LW, UK
UKHW021406190726
13845UKWH00028B/919

9 789334 298512